HOMAGE
TO
THE MAHATMA

HOMAGE TO THE MAHATMA

PUBLICATIONS DIVISION
MINISTRY OF INFORMATION AND BROADCASTING
GOVERNMENT OF INDIA

First Published : 1948
First Reprint : 1949
Second Reprint : January 1998 (Magha 1909)
Revised Edition - 2005 (Saka 1926)

ISBN : 81-230-1103-2

Price: Rs. 40.00

Published by the Director, Publications Division,
Ministry of Information and Broadcasting,
Government of India, Patiala House, New Delhi-110 001

Website : http://www.publicationsdivision.nic.in

Editor : Allah Bukhsh

Cover Design : Vasanti Pardeshi

Typeset at : Goswami Graphics, A-1, Indl. Area, Mayapuri, Ph-1, New Delhi-64

Printed at : Sheel Print-N-Pack, D-132, Hosiery Complex, Phase 2, Noida.

PUBLISHER'S NOTE

THE revised edition of 'Homage to the Mahatma' contains several momentous photographic images from the life and times of the Father of the Nation. The volume first published in 1948, continues to attract the attention of readers, worldwide.

SOON after Mahatma Gandhi's assassination in 1948, tributes flowed like torrents - from every nook and corner of the world. Selections from the volumes of innumerable tributes had been a challenging task. The passage of time has proved that the task was well done, in recording these for future generations, in the form of a book.

IT'S a matter of honour to the Publications Division to present this illustrated edition to the readers.

Prof. UMAKANT MISHRA
Director
Publications Division

CONTENTS

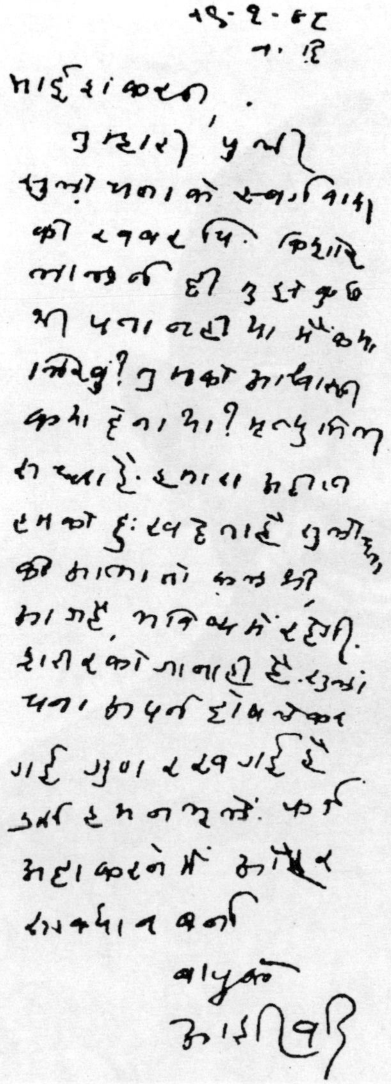

New Delhi

January 29, 1948

Brother Shankaran,

Chi. Kishorlal gave me news of the death of your daughter Sulochana. I had no idea at all of it. What can I write to you? What comfort could I give? Death is a true friend. It is only our ignorance that causes us grief. Sulochana's spirit was yesterday, is to-day and will remain to-morrow. The body, of course, must die. Sulochana has gone taking her failings with her, leaving the good in her behind. Let us not forget that (or her). Be even more true in the discharge of your duty.

With blessings,

BAPU

[A facsimile of one of Gandhiji's last letters, with the English translation alongside]

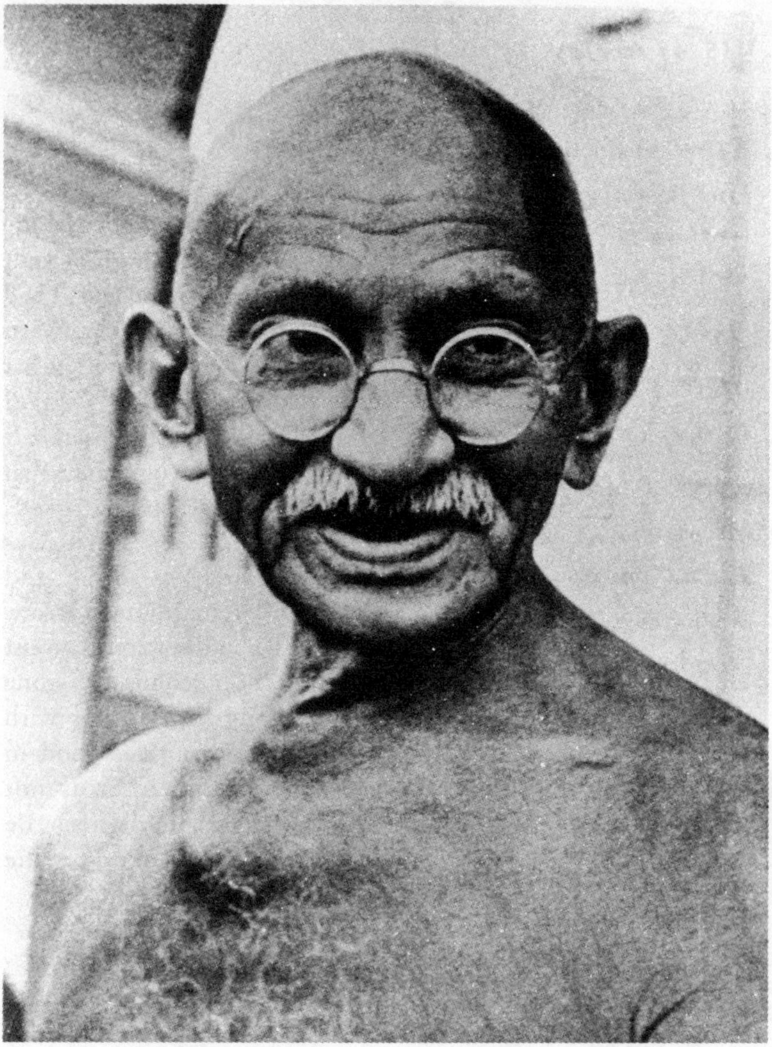

INDIA

Heir to a great tradition Bharatmata is writhing in anguish and pain over the loss. No man loved Bharatmata and Indians more than Mahatma Gandhi. Let the tragedy that was enacted in Delhi give the people of India the tune, reason, rhyme and melody for the history of their future. I pray that the history of India might be written with the rhythm and tune of the grief that Bharatmata had felt when Mahatma Gandhi fell.

No one could die a more glorious death than Mahatma Gandhi. He was going to the seat of his prayer to speak to his Rama. He did not die in a bed calling for hot water, doctors or nurses. He did not die after mumbling incoherent words in the sick bed. He died standing, not even sitting down. Rama was too eager to take him even before he could reach the seat of his prayer.

When Socrates died for his views and Christ for his faith, they believed that they would not get another example like that.

H.E. C. Rajagopalachari, Governor-General

This man of God trod the earth Great men and eminent men have monuments in bronze and marble set up for them, but this man of divine fire managed in his life-time to become enmeshed in millions and millions of hearts so that all of us became somewhat of the stuff that he was made of, though to an infinitely lesser degree. He spread out over India not in palaces only, or in select places, or in assemblies; but in every hamlet and hut of the lowly and those,who suffer. He lives in the hearts of millions and he will live for immemorial ages.

... He has gone, and all over India there is a feeling of having been left desolate and forlorn. All of us sense that feeling, and I do not know when we shall be able to get rid of it, and yet together with that feeling there is also a feeling of proud thanksgiving that it has been given to us of this generation to be associated with this mighty person. In ages to come, centuries and may be millenniums after us, people will think of this generation when this man of God trod the earth and will think of us who, however small, could also follow his path and probably tread on that holy ground where his feet had been. Let us be worthy of him. Let us always be so.

Pandit Jawaharlal Nehru, Prime Minister

His supreme sacrifice will quicken our conscience For even though his mortal frame will turn into ashes tomorrow at 4 p.m., Gandhiji's imperishable teachings will abide with us. I even feel that Gandhiji's immortal spirit is still hovering over us and will continue to watch over the nation's destiny in future also. The mad youth who killed him was wrong if he thought thereby he was destroying his noble mission. Perhaps God wanted Gandhiji's mission to fulfil and prosper through his death.

I am sure Gandhiji's supreme sacrifice will wake up the conscience of our countrymen and evoke a higher response in the heart of every Indian. I hope and pray that it may be given to us to complete Gandhiji's mission. At this solemn moment, no one of us can afford to waver or lose his or her heart. Let us all stand united and bravely face the national disaster that has overtaken us. Let us all solemnly pledge ourselves afresh to Gandhiji's teachings and ideals.

Sardar Vallabhbhai Patel, Deputy Prime Minister

Carried burden of humanity on his frail shoulders Mahatma Gandhi has carried on his frail shoulders a great deal of the burden of humanity and now it was for them to stand together and share it. If millions of Indians could divide that burden and carry it successfully, it would be nothing short of a miracle.

Maulana Abul Kalam Azad, Education Minister

Teacher, seer and prophet We know him as our General, our Guide and the Father of our Nation. To the world at large, he was a teacher, seer and prophet. He gave to mankind a lesson which was as unique as it was sublime. In a world torn asunder by wars, hatred, suspicion and fear, Gandhiji came with his message of love for fellowman. To him true conquest was not the conquest of the battle-field but the conquest of self.

Sardar Baldev Singh, Defence Minister

Undying influence The light that illumined our motherland and indeed the world amidst darkness and sorrow has suddenly gone out. The passing away of Mahatma Gandhi is the most stunning blow that could fall on India. That he who had made India free and self-reliant, a friend of all and enemy of none, loved and respected by millions, should fall at the hands of an assassin, one of his own community and countrymen, is a matter of the deepest shame and tragedy. He is of those whose influence never dies and indeed shines more and more with the passage of time.

The shot of the assassin not only vitally pierced through his mortal body but has grievously struck the very heart of Humanism and India, which could survive only if people resolutely decide to make the pursuit of such methods impossible.

Dr S. P. Mookerjee, Minister for Industry and Supply

He stood between us and disaster It is impossible to estimate his loss at this critical juncture in our history. I am sure that we shall miss his wise counsel more and more as the days pass by. He has led us faultlessly to our goal of political independence: The communal strife that started almost immediately after August 15 wounded him to the depths. An India wedded to violence he could not tolerate.

He saw the moral deterioration in us and, as a loving father, he again unwearyingly pointed out to us the right way. With his infinite love he was trying to quench the anger that raged in many breasts. He was the one thing that stood between us and disaster, for lawlessness and disorder and hate and violence can lead nowhere else.

Rajkumari Amrit Kaur, Health Minister

Made the Harijan cause his own He made the Harijan cause his own and compelled the Congress to adopt it as an integral part of its programme. It was the mission of his life to purge Hinduism of this evil and to remove this blot from its face.

Jagjivan Ram, Labour Minister

Spiritual inspirer and prophet He will occupy in the lives of millions of men a position of a spiritual inspirer and prophet and his reinterpreted message of unattached action will be the guide for the daily conduct of numberless men and women in this land of ours as also other lands.

Jairamdas Daulatram, Food Minister

Considered all men equal He considered all men equal. To him Muslims, Hindus, Sikhs, Parsees, Christians, Jews and all others were human beings, and he fought for their treatment as such.

N. V. Gadgil, Minister for Works, Mines and Power

Gave his country its freedom and its flag Mahatma Gandhi, whose frail body was committed to the flames yesterday, is not dead. It was right that the cremation took place in the midst of the dead kings who were buried in Delhi, for he was the kingliest of all kings. It is right also that he who was the Apostle of Peace should have been taken to the cremation ground with all the honours of a great warrior. Far greater than all warriors who led armies to battle was this little man, the bravest, the most tried friend of all. Delhi has become the centre and the sanctuary of the great revolutionary who emancipated his enslaved country from foreign bondage and gave to it its freedom and its flag.

Mrs Sarojini Naidu, Governor of the United Provinces

Apostle of truth, love and peace He was the most shining embodiment and apostle of truth, love and peace of our age. His spirit is immortal and shall continue to beam upon the dark path of the misguided among mankind.

Personally, I am stunned by overwhelming grief after a life-time of association with him and his mission which, however, demands that one should rededicate oneself to the task for which he lived and died. That can be the only tribute to his memory.

Asaf Ali, Governor of Orissa

The purest spiritual flame in the world Not only has our light gone out, but the purest spiritual flame in the world has been extinguished, especially at a time when its radiance and warmth were at their highest. He was affectionately called "Bapu". More millions have been truly orphaned by his passing away than by that of any other figure in recorded history.

Syud Hossain, India's Ambassador to Egypt

His standards await consummation If we had carried out what he had preached before, he would not have been the victim of this crime. The whole world is shaken.

We must spend the rest of our lives, trying in some small measure to consummate the standards he set.

Mahatma Gandhi's contribution cannot be measured in our age, but since he is dead, we shall try to contribute to the ideals and doctrines he preached.

V.K. Krishna Menon, High Commissioner for India in UK

Whom will we go to now? To us who have worked under him for so many years the news is unbelievable. We used to ask for his advice on everything. We used to ask him to advise us not only on our country's political matters but also on our personal problems. Whom will we go to now?

Sri Prakasa, Indian Higb Commissioner in Pakistan

He had the outlook of humanity There is no sphere of our life in which the hand and influence of the Mahatma are not seen and felt. He gave a new orientation to our politics, our economics, our education and strove for spiritualising everything in our public life. He was the greatest Man of our age. He always had the love of humanity burning in his heart even amidst the darkest periods of hatred and violent struggles and was never a pessimist even when he knew that his voice was a solitary one. Such an unshaken faith in his own principles and mission was naturally a source of strength to us.

We lose him at a very critical time, not only in the history of our country but perhaps in the history of the World. He had the outlook of humanity, international brotherhood and "one world". We have no words to express all that we respect, love, feel and mourn about him.

G. V. Mavlankar, Speaker, Constituent Assembly

The liberator of the Hindu community Can we ever dream that Gandhiji was bringing harm to the Hindus or to their religion? Was it ever possible that this liberator of the Hindu community and emancipator of the low and downtrodden could even think of doing so? But men with narrow minds and limited vision who do not understand the core of Hindu Dharma thought it otherwise and the present calamity is a direct result of such an outlook.

Dr Rajendra Prasad, President, Indian Constituent Assembly

His faith stood the test His death only proves that the world is not yet ready for his doctrine of truth and ahimsa as applied by him to individual and group life. The way of truth and non-violence is yet the way of martyrdom as it has been throughout history.

His faith in the moral law was most seriously tried by recent events, yet he stood the test. His faith did not falter in the darkest hour of his life. Gandhiji always held that the rigour of the moral law required that one must magnify one's own faults and those of one's community and minimise the faults of others and of other communities. It is only thus that the moral law can be truly fulfilled, and when so fulfilled the results must be good. The man and the nation that work in the light of this moral law can never come to grief. Where there is Dharma, ultimate victory is assured.

Acharya J.B. Kripalani, ex-President of the Indian National Congress

Laid down his life for Hindu-Muslim unity It is extremely painful to learn that Mahatma Gandhi was shot dead. He was an embodiment of truth and non-violence and it is due to his sacrifice that India at last achieved freedom.

He laid down his life for Hindu-Muslim unity. His great deeds will be ever remembered in the history of India and the whole world.

The Nizam of Hyderabad

Almost alone among humanity Almost alone among humanity, during a period when war and the havoc of war had benumbed the faculties of man in many ways, Mahatma Gandhi stood up as an apostle of peace and non-violence. The courage that enabled him to preach these doctrines firmly and unequivocally during that period is characteristic of the great sages and seers who, through the ages, have tried to redeem humanity and turn its ways to peace and brotherly love.

The Maharaja of Mysore

The greatest man of our time Gandhiji is no more with us but his spirit and memory will remain with us for ever to inspire and guide us. I and my people join in paying homage to the immortal memory of the greatest man of our time.

The Maharaja of Patiala

Simple as a child Simple as a child, illuminated by the clear light of truth, fortified by the faith in his Creator which moves mountains, loving the country which gave him birth with a passionate tenderness, he went through life giving to others all he had to give and asking for nothing in return. Not his country alone but the whole world has felt the influence of his saintly life and divine mission.

The Nawab of Bhopal

Instilled dignity and self-respect Gandhiji raised politics to a high moral level. He instilled into us a sense of dignity and self-respect. He kindled in us the flame of patriotism and made us realise and become conscious of the heritage of the past. Within a generation, he achieved a miracle.

M. C. Chagla, Chief Justice of Bombay

The light will burn on I would have preferred silence in the face of these circumstances that surround us. For, any words we can find fall flat amid such happenings.

This much, however, I will say, that the light which led us to freedom, though not yet to unity, still burns and will burn on, till it conquers. I believe firmly that a great and united future is the destiny of the nation and its peoples.

The power that brought us through so much struggle and suffering to freedom will achieve also, through whatever strife or trouble, the aim which so poignantly occupied the thoughts of the fallen leader at the time of his tragic ending: as it brought us freedom, it will bring us unity.

A free and united India will be there, and the Mother will gather around her sons and weld them into a single national strength in the life of a great and united people.

Sri Aurobindo

The lonely symbol of a vanishing past I am shocked beyond words at this fatal attack on Gandhiji. The incredible, the inconceivable, has happened. That this purest, most elevating, most inspiring man of our age should have suffered by a madman's anger shows that we have not improved since the days of Socrates, who had to drink hemlock, of Jesus, who was put on the cross.

Mahatma Gandhi, the lonely symbol of a vanishing past, is no more. We have killed his body but the light in him, which is from the divine flame of Truth and Love, cannot be put out.

When will the world be safe for the saints? May the two Dominions, may the whole world, learn that if we are not to slide into the abyss of violence, cruelty and chaos, there is no other way than that for which Mahatma Gandhi has lived and died.

Dr S. Radhakrishnan

Has left a permanent impress on the minds and lives of humanity There can be little doubt that the spontaneous tribute of sorrow and reverence that his martyrdom has evoked from all parts of the world is in essence a recognition and a reciprocation of Mahatma Gandhi's own fundamental humanitarianism which transcended the limits of caste or creed or race or country. Asia has produced other such great humanitarians in the past whose lives have left behind a permanent impress on the minds and lives of humanity.

Sir C. V. Raman

Sacrificed his life for Indian unity I am stunned to hear this tragic news. The noblest man, the greatest patriot and the father of Indian independence has sacrificed his life for the sake of Indian unity. I hope those of the Congressmen who are left behind will prove worthy of him and his traditions. The country is overwhelmed all over but even now let us act in the traditions of Mahatma Gandhi.

Sir Tej Bahadur Sapru

Brothers in martyrdom This foul assassination of the Mahatma marks the climax of the similarity which he valued so dearly between his mission and that of Jesus Christ. They are brothers in martyrdom.

Dr M.R. Jayakar

When comes such another? The country is orphaned and God alone knows what is in store for it. Mahatmaji is dead. When comes such another?

Sarat Chandra Bose

Kashmir will follow him for ever Although Gandhiji is no more, Kashmir will follow him for ever. Kashmiris are laying down their lives for Gandhiji's ideals. As long as a single Kashmiri is alive, the torch of truth and unity lit by Gandhiji will burn brightly.

Sheikh Abdullah

The greatest benefactor of India It was Mahatma Gandhi who, practising truth, patience, perseverance, forbearance and tolerance conducted the nation's peaceful and nonviolent struggle for freedom to success. He was an ardent supporter and upholder of democracy, fraternity and Hindu—Muslim unity, and staked his life several times for his high ideals and at last sacrificed his life for these.

The Working Committee fully appreciates the grand and unparalleled services of the Mahatma to the country as a whole and regards him as the greatest benefactor of India.

Resolution passed by the Working Committee of the Jamiat-ul-Ulema-i-Hind

Actions based on bed-rock of moral values For all of us who joined the struggle for Indian freedom Gandhiji will ever remain the source and inspiration of national service. All his actions were based upon the bed-rock of moral values: it is thus that he achieved the miracle of welding the diverse elements of our national life into a new unity. He lifted our struggle for freedom on to a plane of international peace and translated it in terms of the well-being of the little villager. He provided India with a yardstick by which all social policy may be judged.

National Executive of the Socialist Party

Zealous champion of women's cause Gandhiji served the women of India with a singular zeal. He had taken great pains in raising their status. Women who had never gone out of their homes and had no idea of nationalism came out and joined his movements. Was it not a miracle?

Bapu has put before us two ideals, truth and non-violence. Only posterity knows how far we will succeed in imbibing them. The third thing Bapu wanted us to do was to wipe out communalism.

Kamaladevi Chattopadhyaya

We must follow the path shown by him It is not the time to speak as it is an occasion of mourning. Let us weep. Let the nation weep and wipe off from its soul the stain of the innocent blood of the greatest man the world has ever produced.

We must follow the path shown by Mahatma Gandhi. He came to Delhi with a specific mission, either to do or die. He did a lot and in the end he laid down his life for what he wished to do. Let us now accomplish the sacred task that has been left undone by him.

Jayaprakash Narayan, Socialist Leader

Such a great man is born only once in many centuries By the Mahatma's death the cause of suffering humanity, of world peace and of social justice has received a serious setback. He has died as martyr to the cause of communal harmony and democracy for which he worked all his life. The Father of the Nation has met with a glorious death which he devoutly wished for. His martyrdom is the crowning glory of a noble and divine life nobly lived for his people. Such a great man is born only once in many centuries.

Acharya Narendra Dev

Satyagraha and the Prophet of Arabia I find that the great love of truth in the satyagraha movement has parallels 1,300 years ago. Who does not know who has read the history of our great Prophet of Arabia that he practised what is now termed satyagraha while he was preaching the new religion of Islam in the streets of Mecca? The fact that Mahatina Gandhi in his prayer meetings used to have recitations from the Quoran clearly demonstrated the breadth of his outlook, his sincere endeavour to bring into one whole the different religious-minded people of this sub-continent of India.

The best demonstration of homage to this great man would be to follow in his footsteps in all humbleness and implement his utterances.

Sir Mohammed Saadullah, ex-Premier of Assam

Loss to Muslim world We achieved independence because of Mahatmaji's unceasing efforts all through his life. He fought hard to ameliorate the condition of Indians at large and his untimely and sudden death is indeed a loss to the Muslim world as a whole and has cast gloom all over the world.

Maulvi Abdulla Nurul Haq

He never failed us To him we had learnt to turn for guidance and for advice in all our difficulties, and he never failed us.

Weep India, weep until thy heart breaks, for extinguished is the light that shed truth and justice, a deep love for humanity and transcendental sympathy for the forlorn and the friendless.

I am sure he sees what we do; let us try to fulfil his cherished dream of Hindu-Muslim unity and oneness of mind and spirit in the common service of humanity.

H.S. Suhrawardy, ex-Premier of Bengal

Personified the essence of true religion Gandhiji personified in himself not merely the spirit of India but also the essence of true religion. Religion has many dialects and complexions but Gandhiji spoke its inner voice—of truthfulness, of social justice, of compassion, of tolerance. We have enough religion nowadays to hate one another but Gandhiji had enough religion to love even his enemies.

We cannot all be Gandhis, but we could in a lesser or greater degree imbibe the essence of his teachings, the deeper truths for which he lived and died.

G.L. Mehta

Greatest advocate of Muslim cause In his activities in South Africa and in India, Mahatma Gandhi was more a leader of Muslims than of Hindus. He was the greatest advocate of the cause of Muslims, and tried, and tried successfully, to show them the right path. Had Mahatma Gandhi lived a few years more, he would have been able to bring peace, mutual friendship, and affection between Hindus and Muslims, not only in the Indian Union but also in Pakistan. It was a pity that Providence did not permit him to go to Pakistan. If he had had the chance of going there, the whole set-up of the country would have been changed.

A. R. Siddiqi

Achievements greater than those of kings and saints No king, no saint, no man of any kind could achieve for India what Mahatma Gandhi achieved. In this huge country, geographically, politically and religiously so diverse, he created a unity of ideals. The elevation of his spirit was India's most powerful link.

Sir Girja Shanker Bajpai

Died in the cause of peace As two unofficial Britons living in India, may we express, on behalf of many others of our countrymen here, our deepest sympathy with the people of India in this moment of grief at the martyrdom of this, her great son, who has died in the cause of peace..

Sir Maurice Gwyer, Vice-Chancellor of Delhi University and Arthur Moore, former Editor of The Statesman

Warrior, prophet and saint Seldom, I think, human history records of one individual who was at once a warrior, a prophet and a saint and yet deeply humble and intensely human.

It is this quality of all-embracing human warmth which stands out most prominent in his character.

G.D. Birla

Man of destiny Gandhi, the man of destiny, born to emancipate his country, first emancipated himself by the conquest of desire and fear. He is the saint who became hero in life and martyr in death. He is the modern Messiah of a world torn asunder by war and violence. If it is true, as has been said, that "there was but one Christian and he died on the Cross", it may with equal truth be stated that there was but one Christian and he has been shot. Few people have the glory of writing their own epitaphs. Gandhi, however, has unwittingly left his own, when on March 30, 1931, he stated at Karachi, "Gandhi dies but Gandhism lives for ever."

Dr Pattabhi Sitaramayya,
President, Indian National Congress

Unique in world's history Very rarely in the world's history has a nation's destiny been so inextricably linked with that of a single individual as has been the case with Gandhi and India.

Sir C.P. Ramaswami Aiyar

Architect of Indian freedom The greatest man of the age and among the few of the greatest in world's history, the architect of Indian freedom and the Father of the Nation.

Alladi Krishnaswamy Iyer

Lessons of his life emphasised in his sad demise We have lost the Father of the Nation and no member of the family can feel more agony than the children of this land.

Mahatmaji had indeed been a new Messiah to this world. This martyr-saint even through the method of his sad demise has emphasised the lessons of his life.

Sir Ramaswami Mudaliar, Dewan of Mysore

One of mankind's outstanding sons We join Indians throughout the world in mourning the loss of one of mankind's outstanding sons.

Dr G.M. Naicker, President of the Natal Indian Congress

Greatest man of the present times He was the greatest man of the present times. The services he rendered for the freedom of the country have rarely been rendered by anyone else.

Giani Kartar Singh

One of the greatest reformers and nation-builders of the world When the present dust and heat of political controversy shall have abated in the fullness of time, the historian of the future will justly claim for Mahatmaji the position of one of the greatest reformers and nation-builders of the world.

Dr Sachchidananda Sinha

A great light It is as if a great light has been extinguished and the pain one feels is increased by the anxiety for the future that has become dark.

For me it is one of the greatest catastrophies that could happen to the world we live in. Gandhiji belongs to all men of heart and hope. It is as if a great light had been extinguished but Gandhiji's memory is immortal and lives.

M.C.F. Baron, Governor of French India

The Messiah of this age Mahatma Gandhi was the Messiah of this age. At a time when India was bound with limitations of all kinds, the Mahatma put new life in it and created for it once again a place of honour in the world.

Pandit Govind Ballabh Pant, Premier of UP

Inspiring teachings It is a great loss and to me, it is more than the loss of a father. I personally feel that my life would not have been what it is today but for the inspiration which I have received from his teachings.

Gopi Nath Bardoloi, Premier of Assam

He lives and watches our fumbling efforts May God give us the strength to live up to the teachings of the Great Master, at whose feet we had come together and sat due to some *punya* of our previous births! Tears rush to the eyes at the thought that never more shall we hear that loving, soothing voice; never more shall we feel that magic touch of his pat, which always made one feel strong and lightened one's burden, whether physical or mental. But we must not allow our emotion to be depleted by them. The agony that we all feel at our loss must be transmuted into action. We followed him with halting footsteps during his life-time. Let us all pray that we may be able to do so now with firmness and determination.

Within my heart I hear an echo say: "No, he is not dead. He lives and watches our fumbling efforts with the same old, sweet, sad smile."

Dr Sushila Nayyar, a member of Gandhiji's Ashram

Full of love and gentleness Bapu lived and died for us all—every man, woman and child. He lived, working unceasingly, and died a martyr's death, that we might be turned from the evil path of hatred, greed, violence and untruth.

Bapu was full of love and gentleness, but in his fight with evil he was relentless.

Bapu could fight evil without, because he had mastered the evil within.

Mira Ben (Miss Slade), a member of Gandhiji's Ashram

He completely eschewed hatred A more perfect ideal of *ahimsa* and love cannot be conceived. Gandhiji utilised every evil happening to test his inner purity.

Whether in the form of judicial punishment while dealing with internal crime or in the form of war while dealing with foreign aggression, *himsa* is inevitable in political life. But our apostle of *ahimsa* tried to transform even that unavoidable *himsa* into *ahimsa* by completely eschewing hatred from it.

His Holiness Sri Sankaracharya of Sri Kamakoti Peetah

A solitary and yet shining beacon In a world torn by strife and ridden by bitterness, suspicion and hatred, his voice and teachings stood out almost as a solitary and yet shining beacon pointing the way back to world sanity, love and brotherhood.

Frank Anthony, President, All-India Anglo-Indian Association

I had long ceased to look upon him as my father During the past few months that he was in Delhi it was the privilege of my three-year old boy to be lovingly fondled by Bapu. I was a complete back number and once recently he told me that he missed Gopu more than me whenever we failed to turn up at Birla House. The little urchin now draws renewed tears from our eyes when he pouts his lips in imitation of the way his grandfather greeted him. And yet Gandhiji's interest in the narrow domestic circle was of the meagrest, and I had long ceased to look upon him as my father in any possessive sense. He was to me a saint as much as to any of you and I feel and see the void exactly as you do.

I, therefore, view the disaster with the detachment of one living in the North Pole and having ties neither of blood nor of race with the Great One of whose loss we are as yet but dimly aware.

Devadas Gandhi

The greatest Christian saint At a Christian conference when the president, in the course of his address, asked, "Who is the greatest Christian saint?" none answered. And he announced that it was Mahatma Gandhi. Though a Hindu, by his firm faith in the fatherhood of God and brotherhood of man, he has revealed to us the Kingdom of God which our Lord Jesus came to establish on earth. Jesus said, "When a man loves God and loves man he enters the Kingdom of God." Gandhi has exemplified this in his life and work and has sacrificed his life for his countrymen. He was, we all know, deeply influenced by the Sermon on the Mount.

P. Gurushanta, Bishop of Mysore

A tremendous loss The world has suffered a tremendous loss and lost a great source of inspiration. Gandhiji is dead but the great and noble principles for which he stood and gave up his very life will remain. The fittest homage that we can pay to that great soul is by living up to his noble ideals.

Mir Laik Ali, ex-Prime Minister of Hyderabad

India has lost her soul I feel deeply that tonight India has lost her soul. Mahatmaji was a saint and now that he has departed from our midst, we poor mortals are left without his guidance in a world full of dangers. I hope and pray that my countrymen will keep alive the memory of our beloved leader by living up to his ideals.

Nawab of Chhatari, ex-Premier of Hyderabad

In life a mighty rebel; in death a beacon light No man in recorded history ever lived a life more daring in its conception, more eventful in its import and more human in its urges and impulses. Here is a tragic occasion when one can say truthfully that the world is poorer today, poorer not merely by the passing of this greatest man of the age but by the circumstances in which a life of selfless dedication has been so cruelly and so wantonly cut short.

...In life Gandhiji was a mighty rebel, in death Gandhiji is humanity's beacon light.

Amrita Bazar Patrika, Allahabad

He stood for humanitarian principles Mahatma Gandhi did not belong to India alone; he stood for elemental principles essential to the welfare of humanity as a whole.

Here was a man whose eyes were opened to the tribulations of his people generations ago in a far-off land; who from that day onwards gave his mind—and now literally his body—to their salvation. How far Mahatma Gandhi's devotion to things of the spirit in the greatest and most influential tradition of the East will prove of lasting and immortal consequence must largely depend on the extent to which those of this generation and others immediately following are inspired by his precepts and his memory.

The Times of India, Bombay

He provided alternative to atomic warfare Mahatma Gandhi was not merely a great nationalist but perhaps a greater internationalist, proving by action that the two are not incompatible. He was unique in evolving, and in rendering world-famous, a weapon novel in modern times with which to fight, the weapon of non-violence. The world may soon find it has no alternative, because of the horrifying new means of slaughter now developed.

Whether the nations come to their senses in time, or are engulfed in atomic war, Mahatma Gandhi will stand pre-eminent in this century as the man who not only saw, before most others, the calamitous objectives to which violence of its nature tends, but who made practical efforts on an unprecedentedly large scale to provide an alternative.

The Statesman, Calcutta

Born to refashion a new civilisation Mahatma Gandhi was born to refashion a new civilisation and make the people of India the vehicle of that civilisation. No span of individual mortal life–long as it was by the mercy of Providence—could suffice for anything more than laying the foundations. With the disappearance of his physical body it has become the glorious destiny of his country and his people to build upon the foundations he has laid a structure of which he as well as humanity may be proud.

The Hindustan Times, New Delhi

A life of service to all The hundreds and thousands of messages which keep the wires and radio of the world vibrating at the moment show how deeply Gandhiji has impressed humanity as an apostle of peace and as one who has been rightly hailed as the world's Second Saviour. No wonder so many leaders of thought in Europe and America have been profoundly struck and influenced by his ideas of plain living and high thinking, of non-violence even in the face of extreme provocation and life of service to all.

The Hindu, Madras

His peculiar greatness In the political history of mankind, there have been many towering personalities who have passed into legend, some into oblivion: But the peculiar greatness of this man lay in his being a type by himself, the like of which the world has never seen.

He was the one complete man in this age of errors. He combined in a single self the multiple roles of saint, philosopher, politician and guide. Time will bring out in sharp relief his true greatness in relation to others. His achievement was little short of miracle.

Reshadat K.H. Moula (from a letter in The Statesman)

The loss to Muslims, particularly those who have made India their home, is irreplaceable. The Mahatma sacrificed his life to save them. We shall never forget.

Ali Ben Yusuf (from a letter in The Statesman)

Sudden revelation Today, Gandhiji's death is more than a momentary spell. It is a shock which has sprung, not from the sudden close of his life, but from the sudden display of what his life was. So it must have expression in the career of the world, not a mere impression on the mind of an individual nation.

M. Rama Doss (from a letter in The Illustrated Weekly of India)

The duty of renunciation differentiates mankind from the beast.

There is no deliverance and no hope without sacrifice, discipline and self-control.

-Mahatma Gandhi

WALK ALONE

If they answer not to thy call, walk alone,
  If they are afraid and cower mutely facing the wall;

O thou of evil luck,
  Open thy mind and speak out alone.

If they turn away, and desert you
when crossing the wilderness

  O thou of evil luck,

Trample the thorns under thy tread,
  and along the blood-lined track travel alone.

If they do not hold up the light
  When the night is troubled with storm

O thou of evil luck,
  With the thunder-flame of pain ignite thine own heart

And let it burn alone.

(A song by Tagore, favourite with Gandhiji)

PAKISTAN

A noble death I associate myself with the tributes that have been paid to this great man.

He died in the discharge of the duty in which he believed. His tragic death, however much we may deplore it and however much we may condemn the murderer, was a noble death, for he died in the discharge of his duty.

Quaid-i-Azam M.A. Jinnah

Died when most needed I am shocked to hear the news. The greatest tragedy is that when Mahatma Gandhi was most needed he has been taken away from us.

India has lost one of her greatest sons and history will record it as one of the blackest crimes committed.

Khwaja Nazimuddin, Governor-General, Pakistan

Memorable efforts for communal harmony His removal from the stage of Indian politics at this juncture is an irreparable loss.

His great effort for the restoration of communal harmony will be remembered with gratitude by all lovers of peace and goodwill. We earnestly hope that his efforts for communal harmony—which he had foremost in his heart just before his tragic death—will be crowned with success.

Liaquat Ali Khan, Prime Minister

Stunned every lover of peace The news of Gandhiji's assassination has stunned evey lover of peace. That a great man who preached non-violence should die a violent death is highly tragic.

During the last few months Gandhiji was devoting his entire attention to the cause of communal unity and understanding. Let us hope and pray that his tragic death will not weaken the hands of forces that are working for communal harmony and peace.

Ghulam Mohammed, Finance Minister

Changed the course of modern history The news of the assassination was one of those personalities who have contributed materially in changing the course of modern history. He was gifted with the unique power of mobilising public opinion on any question. He created political consciousness in the sub-continent of India in a remarkable and unprecedented manner.

His death at the hands of a Hindu assassin should arouse in both Hindus and Mussalmans a consciousness of the danger latent in the cancer of communal bitterness and lead them to cement bonds of friendship between them.

I.I. Chundrigar

Champion of the weak Mahatma Gandhi will go down in history as a most ardent friend of the weak and the injured.

He has given his life for a noble cause which was dearest to his heart after the achievement of independence, namely, the protection of the Muslim minority in India. Muslims in India today are the worst sufferers by his passing...

Ghazanfar Ali Khan

Harbinger of peace He was the harbinger of peace and pioneer of constructive activities.

Sheikh Karamat Ali, Education Minister

He gave his life for humanity It would surely be true to say that he gave his life for humanity. He was sacrificed because he had the courage to proclaim the brotherhood of man in circumstances in which less magnanimous souls emphasize hostility and hatred.

Such a death can never be in vain. What he achieved in life we all know. It remains for us to ensure that what he stood for in death shall illumine the road new India is to follow.

Sir Frederick Bourne, Governor of East Bengal

Noblest teacher In him India and humanity have lost their noblest teacher, who even in his old age and in weak health, carried on with energy and conviction his peace mission with unrivalled courage. Indian Muslims especially had in him a true friend and their loss is very heavy indeed.

Zahid Hussain, former Pakistan High Commissioner in India

Martyr to a great cause One of the greatest figures of the world of today has passed away. He fought most valiantly for peace between Hindus and Muslims and between the two nations, and fell a martyr to a great cause. Humanity has lost one of the most dynamic personalities. Undoubtedly he will live long in history. Let us hope that in death he will achieve what he could not while living.

Khan Abdul Qaiyum Khan, Premier, NWFP

The greatest leader for centuries I was deeply shocked to hear the tragic news of the assassination of Mahatma Gandhi, the greatest leader India has produced for many centuries. His efforts for the restoration of peace had attracted world-wide attention. He will, I am certain, live in the hearts of all peace lovers and though he may not be in our midst his spirit will continue to guide those who are anxious for the return of genuine peace.

Khan Iftikhar Hussain of Mamdot, Premier of West Punjab

One of the greatest men in history Gandhiji was undoubtedly one of the greatest men the world has ever produced. He struggled for freedom through non-violent means, but it is indeed tragic that he was assassinated.

He tried after August 15 to maintain communal harmony and peace, and his great work in Delhi can never be forgotten. Unfortunately, he did not complete his mission, but we hope that what he has left undone will be done by the peoples of India and Pakistan and that the minorities will be protected throughout the sub-continent and that his ideals will ever be cherished.

Khuhro, ex-Premier of Sind

The greatest tragedy since Karbala The assassination of Mahatma Gandhi is one of the most tragic events since the great tragedy of Karbala. It is impossible to find words to express the feelings that are uppermost in our minds. May his soul rest in peace.

A.K. Fazlul Huq, ex-Premier of Bengal

He was the only ray of light to help us through these darkest days.

Khan Abdul Ghaffar Khan, Red Shirt Leader

He lived and died for peace The news of the Mahatma's demise has come as a great shock. He lived for peace and he died for peace. His trust in God was his great shield against all dangers to his life. I am sure his mission for peace is not dead. Providence will, through its own strange ways, carry on that work to the satisfaction of the Mahatma's great soul.

Firoz Khan Noon

Those who have any doubt about his sincerity were fully convinced by his last fast that he wanted above everything else the establishment of complete cordiality between Hindus and Muslims of India and Pakistan.

Dr M. Hassan, Vice-Chancellor, Dacca University

The greatest servant of humanity who gave his life in the cause of human service... His efforts to create unity, love and affection between Hindus and Muslims will be hailed by the entire world.

The Pir of Manki Sharif

An epoch ends Mahatma Gandhi's death ends an epoch of Indian history of which he was the originator... Each one of us who has raised his hand against innocent men, women and children during the past months, who has publicly or secretly entertained sympathy for such acts, is a collaborator in the murder of Mahatma Gandhi.

Mian Iftikharuddin, President, West Punjab Muslim League

Timeless symbol of love and rectitude Mahatma Gandhi is dead. The world has been deprived of the sight and sound of his frail body and aged voice—the body and voice that had in the last few months almost lost, for a large section of mankind, their personal and ephemeral character and become timeless symbols of compassionate love and fearless rectitude. In his last momentous days Gandhi, the politician, gave place to the infinitely greater Gandhi, the man.

The best loved and most venerated political leader and moral evangelist of a near sub-continent, the idol of millions, has been publicly murdered. In India and Pakistan today every heart and every conscience should be searched to assess how far every heart and every conscience is answerable for this most fearful of tragedies.

The people of India and indirectly the people of Pakistan, for he was trying to befriend both, have added to their other losses the most grievous loss of all—the loss of Gandhiji.

The Pakistan Times, Lahore

Bulwark of world peace and liberty The greatest man of the modern age, the bulwark of world peace and world liberty, the saint who had dominated our souls for well over a generation, the invincible hero who single-handed and without a weapon defied the might of the British lion, the tried healer of heart's wounds, the magician who made heroes out of clay and carved out an imperishable name for India in the chancelleries of Europe and America, has been removed from our midst.

The Daily Gazette, Karachi

UK

Irreparable loss The Queen and I are deeply shocked by the death of Mr Gandhi. Will you please convey to the people of India our sincere sympathy in the irreparable loss which they, and indeed mankind, have suffered.

His Majesty the King

A divinely inspired saint I know that I am expressing the views of the British people in offering to his fellow-countrymen our deep sympathy in the loss of their greatest citizen. Mahatma Gandhi, as he was known in India, was one of the outstanding figures in the world today, but he seemed to belong to a different period of history.

Living a life of extreme asceticism, he was revered as a divinely inspired saint by millions of his fellow-countrymen. His influence extended beyond the range of his co-religionists.

For a quarter of a century this one man has been the major factor in every consideration of the Indian problem. He had become the expression of the aspirations of the Indian people for independence, but he was not just a nationalist. His most distinctive doctrine was that of non-violence. He believed in a method of passive resistance to those forces which he considered wrong. The sincerity and devotion with which he pursued his objectives are beyond all doubt.

The hand of the murderer has struck him down and a voice which pleaded for peace and brotherhood has been silenced, but I am certain that his spirit will continue to animate his fellow-countrymen and will plead for peace and concord.

Clement Attlee, Prime Minister

A tragic end to the life of a great and remarkable man.

Herbert Morrison, Deputy Prime Minister

Words fail adequately to express what we feel for the loss India and the whole world has sustained in this terrible event.

All of us were watching Mr Gandhi's last efforts with great admiration and when the news came it was a tremendous blow.

Ernest Bevin, Foreign Minister

Left an indelible impression of goodness Mr Gandhi's death is a personal loss for me. I shall never forget the impression of goodness he made on me when I met him in Delhi three weeks ago. I felt I was in the presence of a man of great spiritual power. Coming so closely on the heels of the culmination of the task towards which he had so unsparingly devoted himself for nearly a life-time, his loss is tragic and grievous.

Arthur Henderson, Air Minister

Mr Gandhi was one of the few great towering lives that would stand out in a century of history, for his principles and his adhesion to non-violence in all his work of getting people together.

A. V. Alexander, Defence Minister

We all mourn the passing of a great man whose life has been an example to the world.

Lord Addison, Government Leader in the House of Lords

The most remarkable man of the century. One can only hope that his death will bring the different communities of India into that closer understanding and association to which he devoted the whole of his great life.

Sir Hartley Shawcross, Attorney General

Stood out head and shoulders above contemporaries May not the whole world learn from his life something of fundamental value: that it is idle to try to save ourselves from destruction by the use of force and that our greatest weapon of salvation is the supreme and redeeming power of love.

...Non-violence for him was not a negative policy, it was much more than that. It was the determination that the power of love should triumph, a determination based upon a deep and unshakable belief in that power. He never took the view that he must divorce his religion from his everyday life. Religion was his life and his life was his religion...

He was no simple missionary. Combined with his religious outlook was his lawyer-trained mind, quick and apt for reasoning. He was a formidable opponent for argument and would often take up the attitude that his views and the policy he was advocating had come to him in his meditations from God and then no reasoning upon earth could make him depart from them.

...He stood out head and shoulders above all his contemporaries as one who believed and who fearlessly put his beliefs into practice. I know no other man of any time or indeed in recent history who forcefully and convincingly demonstrated the power of the spirit over material things.

Sir Stafford Cripps, Chancellor of the Exchequer

Universal brother, lover and friend Gandhiji was deeply loved, He will be deeply mourned. He is no longer with us in the flesh, but his spirit endures. What was the secret of his power over the hearts and minds of men and women? In my opinion it was the fact that he voluntarily stripped himself of every vestige of the privilege that he could have enjoyed on account of his birth, means, personality and intellectual pre-eminence and took on himself the status and infirmities of the ordinary man.

When he was in South Africa as a young man and opposed the treatment of his fellow-countrymen in that land, he courted for himself the humiliation of the humblest Indian that he might in his own person face the punishment meted out for disobedience.

When he called for non-cooperation with the British in India he himself disobeyed the law and insisted that he must be among the first to go to prison. When he declaimed against the adoption by India of Western industrialism he installed a spinning wheel in his own house and laboured at it daily with his own hands. When he set out to combat inter-communal violence he faced death by starvation in an act of penance for the error and sin of the community of which he was himself a member.

He never claimed to be any other than an ordinary man. He acknowledged his liability to error and admitted that he had frequently learnt by his mistakes. He was the universal brother, lover and friend of poor, weak, erring, suffering humanity. Let us all do homage to his spirit, not by words alone but by dedicating our lives as he did to the pursuit of truth, the love of our fellow-men, the healing of the wounds of nations.

Lord Pethick-Lawrence, former Secretary of State for India & Burma

His death closes a great chapter in world history All Englishmen, without difference of party, will have deeply regretted the news. It is tragic to think that he who all his life preached communal unity to Indians should himself have fallen a victim to the frenzy of communal passion.

His part in the history of India and Anglo-Indian relations in the last generation can only be assessed by history. At any rate, it can be said that no one contributed more to the particular way in which the charter of British rule in India has ended than Mahatma Gandhi himself.

His death comes at the close of a great chapter in world history. In the mind of India, at least, he will always be identified with the opening of the new chapter which, however troubled at the outset, we should all hope, will develop in peace, concord and prosperity for India.

L.S. Amery, former Secretary of State for India

Even a saint is not safe in our times The death of Mahatma Gandhi is not only terrible in itself but also a sad commentary on the state of our present civilization.

The life of even a saint is no longer safe in our times. This is a direct result of the effects of two world wars and the spread of totalitarianism which has led to a steady berefting from human life of the sanctity which our creed has always placed upon it.

Lord Vansittart, former Chief British Diplomatic Adviser

So wise a counsellor, so kind a friend, so unique a master... Gandhiji was one of those rare beings who represent in the course of their own lives an everlasting struggle between good and evil...The pain and suffering of the world became his suffering...His death will surely prove the last and greatest of his victories.

Lord Listowel

Few like him in all history The news of Mahatma Gandhi's murder is the news of a great tragedy to India and to the cause for which, at anytime, he was willing to give his life.

No one has tried to serve India with greater devotion, and his friends in India and elsewhere will only hope that the lesson and effect of his tragic death may be to bring all his countrymen to understand and practise the principles that he so constantly and faithfully preached.

I suppose there can be few men in all history who, by personal character and example, have been able so deeply to influence the thought of their generation.

Lord Halifax, former Viceroy of India

An irreparable loss to the unity of India. I never imagined he would go out like that; he, an old man, seemed to indicate that he would live a long time.

Lord Wavell, former Viceroy of India

Life of love and truth Gandhiji's death is truly a loss to mankind which so sorely needs the living light of those ideals of love and tolerance for which he strove and died. In her hour of deep sorrow India is proud to have given to the world a man of his imperishable renown and is confident that his example will be a source of inspiration and strength in the fulfilment of her destiny...

India, indeed the world, will not see the like of him again, perhaps, for centuries.

Our one consolation in this hour of unparalleled grief is that his life of truth, toleration and love towards his fellows may inspire our troubled world to save itself by following his noble example.

Lord Mountbatten, former Governor-General of India

An international tragedy The death of Mahatma Gandhi is not only a national disaster, but an international tragedy. My heart is so full that I am unable to find words. Gandhiji's death is a world loss. He was a great leader. The utmost we can do now is to try and carry on and live up to the principles which Gandhiji has taught us.

Countess Mountbatten

If his spirit can prevail, there will be no carnage and explosive hate in India now that his voice is still.

R. Sorensen

He devoted his life to win men from violence to peace and brotherhood. Fanaticism and hatred have now made him a martyr for that cause.

Dr Fisher, Archbishop of Canterbury

Deathless child of God I rejoice to think that Canterbury showed him hospitality at that rather bitter period of his life. I rejoice to think of what he has done for India. Mahatma Gandhi is not dead. Mahatma Gandhi lives. The children of God never die.

Dr Hewlett Johnson, Dean of Canterbury

Gandhiji's efforts to preserve order in the two new Dominions have been acclaimed throughout the peace-loving nations of the world.

Cardinal Griffin, Catholic Primate of England & Scotland

The loss of one whose saintly character and life-long devotion to the cause of peace will cause his name always to be remembered.

D.H.M. Lazarus, Acting Chief Rabbi

It shows how dangerous it is to be too good.

George Bernard Shaw

Greatest figure in history The world has lost its greatest figure—perhaps history too, has lost its greatest figure. I pray that India may act according to the spirit of Mr Gandhi and not that of his assassin and that the whole world will catch his spirit and shall move towards the peace which Mr Gandhi loved.

Fenner Brockway

Friend of the English The long struggle against British power never led to alienation from the English people. Not only did he count several viceroys, and other British rulers as his friends, but even among those who were his close intimates, among those who ran to him with all their problems and difficulties, among those who loved to call him 'Bapu', not a few were Englishmen and women.

Horace G. Alexander of the Society of Friends

He is a light to the whole world.

Dr Gilbert Murray, Oxford

Mr Gandhi's courageous stand for communal co-operation won the admiration of the world and the hatred of communal extremists... The work for which Mr Gandhi gave his life must go forward...

The British Communist Party

His brave campaign The Mahatma did not teach a soft doctrine of complacence but he did, like Jesus Christ, convince millions of people that the only alternative to an endless succession of hates and wars was to realise that truth and love were the supreme methods of warfare, for the only true victory is to turn your enemy into your friend...I was present when Mahatma Gandhi held his prayer meeting at Mehrauli Tomb, as part of his brave and beneficent campaign to end hatred and bitterness between Hindus and Muslims. People sometimes speak as if the western world is incapable of appreciation of such a life as Gandhi's...But they sometimes forget what Gandhi always remembered that Christ himself taught a doctrine that was closely akin to *ahimsa*...

Kingsley Martin, Editor, New Statesman & Nation, London

A high religious tragedy The darkness which is over the earth today is but the deepening of a shadow which has fallen across all generations of men. The murder of Mahatma Gandhi is something far more terrible than any political crime. It belongs to the supernatural realm of high religious tragedy.

The hand that killed the Mahatma is the same hand that nailed the Cross. It is the hand that fired the faggots. It is the hand that through the ages has been growing ever more mighty in war and less sure in the pursuit of peace. It is your hand and mine...

Yet after the work of the Mahatma, it is not too presumptuous to hope for a miracle. It may be that the death of this leader, who was held in so much reverence by so many millions, will raise men to heights they have not hitherto attained. It may be that love against which the gun has no power will evoke out of this great tragedy, the beginnings of peace and unity for India.

Now in the pain of Mahatma Gandhi's death it is possible to realise how lasting and how strong is the faith which he preached. Now we can see that the light which was kindled in the East has not been put out, but is made one with the white radiance of eternity.

The News Chronicle, London

Mahatma Gandhi will rightly take his place alone in Indian history as a leader who embodied far more than his own religious community's ideas of human brotherhood, of respect for individual conscience, and of supreme self-sacrifice in support of right.

The Times, London

To the West he is, above all, the man who revived and refreshed the meaning and value of religion.

The Manchester Guardian

Mahatma Gandhi has lost his life truly as a martyr in the fight against communal conflict...The solemnity of the moment calls for renewed efforts to find the path of co-operation and democratic unity.

The Daily Worker, London

The assassination is not only a calamity for India but for the world. Mahatma Gandhi was one of the great teachers of mankind.

The Daily Herald, Londan

He gave to Indians a new sense of power and responsibility and the value of political agitation.

The Daily Telegraph, London

EUROPE

BELGIUM

His death has plunged into personal mourning all men who have not ceased to believe in the power of the spirit and the radiance of godliness. Let this tragic death continue to serve his noble dream of human fraternity.

Frans Van Cauwelaer, President of the Belgian Chamber of Deputies

CZECHOSLOVAKIA

The representative of your independence and freedom.

Dr Edward Benes

Herald of love, compassion, kindness and brotherhood ....Mahatma Gandhi fought against evil wherever it appeared and even in wartime he did not cease being an apostle of mercy, human brotherhood and peace among nations. The world should listen to its conscience and fulfil Gandhi's legacy, uniting in his spirit.

M. Josef David, Speaker, Czechoslovak National Assembly

He died as a living proof of down-trodden humanity besmirched by political fanatics.

Svobodne Noviny

DENMARK

The fact that Mr Gandhi in his advanced age has been killed immediately after putting his life into the battle for peace in India will, all the civilized world over, be taken as proof of the brutality the last war has created in people's minds.

M. Hedtoft, Premier

Gandhiji's famous march on foot to the seacoast at Dandi on the eve of Salt Satyagraha, 1930.

Arriving at a prayer meeting in New Delhi. With him are Khan Abdul Ghaffar Khan, Jawaharlal Nehru and Acharya Kriplani.

Gandhiji, Sardar Patel and Maniben Patel at Simla where Gandhiji had gone to meet the Viceroy, July 1945.

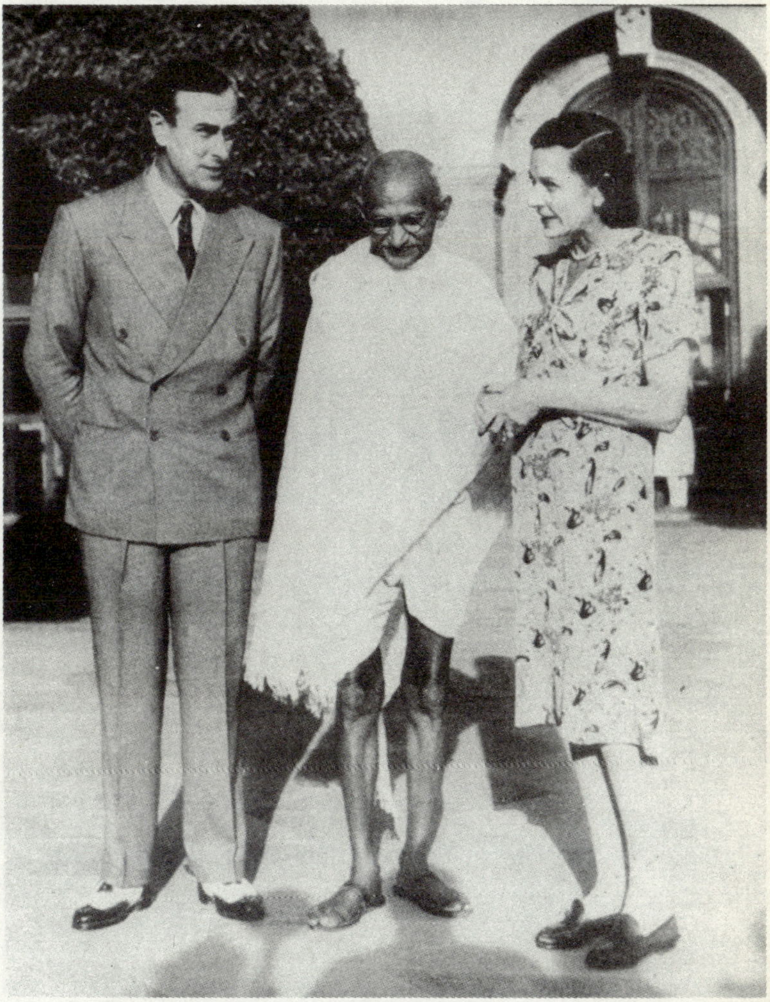

With Lord and Lady Mountbatten.

On way to the communally disturbed Noakhali, East Bengal,
November 1946.

Arriving for the Id-reunion meeting at the Calcutta Maidan, August 1947.

Mahatma's body lying in State at the Birla House, New Delhi.

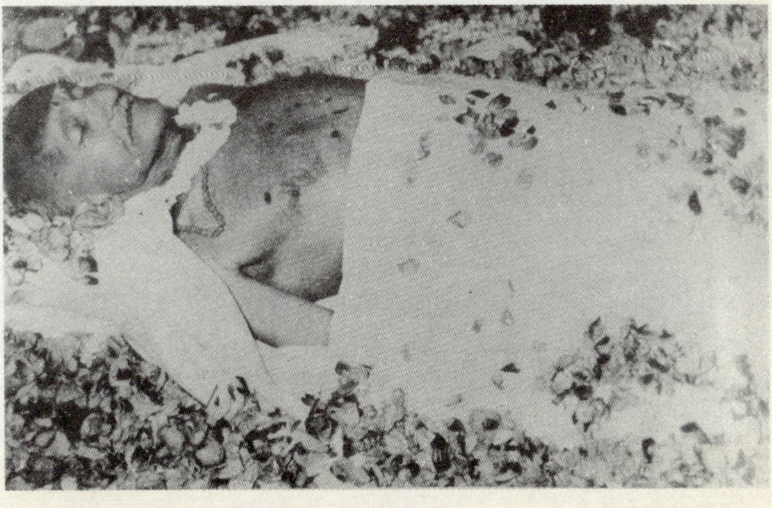

Funeral procession on its way to Rajghat, New Delhi.

Samadhi at Rajghat.

EIRE (Ireland)

His noble life was inspiration to all The people of Ireland, in union with lovers of liberty in all lands, mourn the loss of one whose noble, self-sacrificing life in the service of his country was an inspiration to all.

May it please God to grant to India and the whole world that charity, brotherhood and peace for which he so very earnestly prayed and worked.

Sean O'Kelly, President

The world has lost a great leader I have learned with profound sorrow of the tragic death of Mr Gandhi. The loss is not India's alone. The world has lost a great leader whose influence will long survive his death.

In spite of this grievous loss, we hope that India will not cease to go forward, undiscouraged, to the attainment of the ideals for which Mr Gandhi strove.

de Valera, ex-Premier

FINLAND

Depressed at the tragic death of the great national leader of India, I wish to express my deep sympathy to the family of Mahatma Gandhi.

J.K. Passikivi, President

Please accept the expression of deep sympathy of the Finnish people at the tragic death of Mahatma Gandhi.

Prime Minister

FRANCE

The Republic of France and the people of the Union of France associate themselves with all their heart in the great sorrow which has befallen the Indian Nation.

Prime Minister

France stands at the bier of this great man The world has heard today one of the saddest tidings of our time. He... showed that goodwill and renunciation would conquer hate and ambition. Not only his own people will mourn him, but all those who believe in the possibility of brotherly understanding. Mr Gandhi gave the example of an obstinate, an absolute search for love of mankind, whatever their race or religion. France stands to-night at the bier of this great man, fallen victim to the violence against which he always fought. May his sacrifice crown his life-work.

M. George Bidault, Foreign Minister

May the memory of the Apostle of India inspire men of all races in their march towards liberty and justice and may the idea of mutual understanding prevail over violence and fatalism.

A resolution of the Council of the Republic of France

I never saw Mr Gandhi... I do not know his language. I never set foot in his country and yet I feel the same sorrow as if I had lost someone near and dear. The whole world has been plunged into mourning by the death of this extraordinary man.

Leon Blum in Le Populaire

Gandhi's blood will accomplish the miracle which he had wrought in the last days of his life by his supreme fast. For the victories achieved by calculated violence over obstinate non-violence are always apparent and temporary. The Mahatma will have the last word.

M. Maurice Schuman, in the Popular Republican organ L'Aube

Human element above "isms" Because he believed that fraternity was more efficacious than violence he succumbed to violence. Because he believed that wisdom was more fecund than blind passion, he was struck down by a fanatic. Over and above automatic hatred and prejudice, he was the spirit. Over and above nationalism and imperialism, he was the human element. Is it a sign of the times that he was struck down not in spite of, but on account of this?

L'Aurore, Paris

GERMANY

Mr Gandhi will live on with us as an example of humanity... his influence will be stronger than ever before...

Dr Kurt Schumacher, German Social Democrat Leader

His great soul will continue to live in his people.

Telegraf

GREECE

His loss is as great for mankind as it is for India. The Greek people have always appreciated and admired Gandhiji's greatness.

M. Tsaldaras, Deputy Prime Minister and Minister of Foreign Affairs

ITALY

The great man was the spiritual leader of millions of Indians and had always struggled for peace.

His Holiness Pope Pius XII, Vatican City

Europe invented nationalism. This theory is passing to Asia and Africa, now dripping with blood and stained with crime. Mr Gandhi's murder gives the last touch to the atmosphere of bestiality which is everywhere confusing our generation.

All Italy is with you in the deep sorrow of your loss which is a loss for the whole of mankind.

Count Sforza, Foreign Minister

This peace-loving man This hour, so sad for our civilisation, has, indeed, been darkened by the detestable assassination of Gandhi. In killing this peace-loving man, it seems that an attempt has been made to strike a blow at peace. As in all political crimes these fanatics think that by killing a person they will destroy the faith and ideals he represents. But these crimes have only the very opposite effect. They elevate that faith and those ideals and make them shine out all the more. The truth of this has come in the protests and horror which the murder of Gandhi has raised throughout the world.

Osservatore Romano, Vatican City

The glorious victim of peace of the world.

II Popolo

He was a saint and prophet.

Giornale d'Italia

It was the tragic death of the saint of liberty.

II Risorgimento Liberale

LUXEMBOURG

May the message of peace and liberty for which the Mahatma lived and died remain alive among the nations of the world.

Minister of Foreign Affairs

NETHERLANDS

No personal sacrifice had been too great for the Mahatma's devotion to the welfare of his fellow-men.

Dr Louis Beel, Prime Minister

NORWAY

Inspired life-long work for peace The memory of the Mahatma and of his inspired life-long work for peace and brotherhood amongst men will always live in Norway.

Minister of Foreign Affairs

POLAND

Mahatma Gandhi's high virtues acquired during the fight for democracy and against tyranny have been recognised by the entire world.

Foreign Minister

PORTUGAL

In my own name and in the name of the Portuguese nation, please accept our profound sympathies on the tragic death of Mahatma Gandhi.

President

A great moral figure of the world.

Prime Minister

SWITZERLAND

The Prince of Peace Mahatma Gandhi exceptionally personified the Prince of Peace whose loss affects all liumanity.

President

The Mahatma was the only moral force able to control the turbulence of the two states of the sub-continent in the throes of formation.

La Suisse, Geneva

TURKEY

Mahatma Gandhi's loss is a misfortune which hits the entire humanity.

President, Grand National Assembly

To die at the hands of one's brother is a privilege, provided you die bravely.

-Mahatma Gandhi

USA

A leader of international stature Gandhi was a great Indian nationalist, but at the same time he was a leader of international stature. His teachings and his actions have left a deep impression on millions of people. As a teacher and leader, his influence made itself felt not only in India, but everywhere in the world and his death brings great sorrow to all peace-loving people. Another giant among men has fallen in the cause of brotherhood and peace. I know that the peoples of Asia will be inspired by his tragic death to strive with increased determination to achieve the goals of cooperation and mutual trust for which the Mahatma has now given his life.

President Truman

There is no doubt Gandhi had great spiritual qualities and the one only hope, even though he is not with his people, is that his influence had much of value to give to the rest of the world and one hopes the very violence of his death will turn people away from violence.

Eleanor Roosevelt

Spokesman for the conscience of all mankind The USA has been shocked by the tragic news of the passing of Mahatma Gandhi and shares with India the heavy burden of sorrow and loss. The bereavement felt in this country is the evidence of the close ties between the peoples of USA and India.

Mahatma Gandhi was the spokesman for the conscience of all mankind.

George C. Marshall, former Secretary of State

World better because he lived The world is a better world for his having lived, but the greatness of this extraordinary man will not die with him. The spirit of Mahatma Gandhi will live and grow and his influence will increase with the years. A great human spirit lives on though his body has returned to dust.

Like any great man, he does not belong to India alone. He belongs to all of us everywhere and the one consolation we can take from this tragedy is that his influence and the force of his spiritual personality will be greater now than they were when he lived.

All differences between men and nations can be reconciled. If the spirit is there, the way can always be found. As our own great martyr to world peace, Franklin Roosevelt, said on one occasion, 'It is the spirit, Sir, that matters'. It is the spirit of Mahatma Gandhi, his ideals and dedication to peace everywhere—a peace based on the love of man for man—that matters.

Dr Henry Grady, former US Ambassador to India

Gandhi was one of the deathless few across the centuries, who have lifted human character to immortal authority...who made humility and simple truth more powerful than empires...

Senator Arthur H. Vandenberg, Chairman of the Senate Foreign Relations Committee

A prophet ahead of the times Nothing more revolting has occurred in the history of the modern world than the senseless assassination of this venerable man. That he should die by violence is one of those bitter anachronisms that seems to refute all logic.

In the evolution of civilization, if it is to survive, all men cannot fail eventually to adopt his belief that the process of mass application of force to resolve contentious issues is fundamentally not only wrong but contains within itself the germs of self-destruction.

Gandhiji, however, was one of those prophets who lived far ahead of the times.

General Douglas MacArthur, C-in-C, Allied Forces in Japan

The man who was right Gandhi's death, brought about by one of his own people, is another crucifixion. Our home is not alone in its mourning. All over the country, all over the world, people, who never saw Gandhi in the flesh, mourn him now. He dies at a moment of unique influence.

It was only a few days ago that we were remarking about the rising interest in Gandhi among Americans. He had won great reverence.

Real reverence for Gandhi was embedded in the hearts of the people and it had begun to dawn on us that he was right. Here, in the midst of our mounting militarism, we were beginning to look towards Gandhi as the man who was right. Our newspapers recognised this new force. India won much by this. We were all moved by the struggle led by Gandhi for a peaceful way of settling differences between nations.

Pearl S.Buck

His spirit reached for the stars A great warm light has been extinguished with the death of Gandhi. Gandhi died as he lived, seeking through understanding and compassion and love to absolve the ignorant and bigoted and self-seeking. His convincing gospel saved man in spite of themselves. His spirit reached for the stars and sought to win a world without gun or bayonet or blood. Out of his love of God and his fellow-men, he forged a political weapon. He glorified the chains and jails of his captors into the shining ornaments of martyrdom. Mahatma Gandhi cannot die, his spirit is free to stir men's souls in every corner of the earth. As we, mothers of the earth, stand in awesome fear of the roar of jet planes, the crash of atom bombs and the unknown horrors, of germ warfare, we must turn our eyes in hope to the East where the sun of the Mahatma blazes.

Mary Bethune, American Negro Leader

The brightest beacon to Africans With heavy hearts we join India's sorrow and bow our heads sadly before the mortal remains of the world's greatest humanitarian. Gandhi's life-work will always remain the brightest beacon and inspiration to Africans struggling for freedom and we pray that India's future be worthy of her greatest son.

Joseph Mitchell, George Padmore, Richard Hard (Negro Leaders)

Only statesman to stand for higher human relationship Everyone concerned in the better future of mankind must be deeply moved by the tragic death of Mahatma Gandhi. He died as the victim of his own principles, the principle of non-violence. He died because in time of disorder and general irritation in his country, he refused armed protection for himself. It was his unshakable belief that the use of force is an evil in itself, that therefore it must be avoided by those who are striving for supreme justice to his belief. With his belief in his heart and mind, he has led a great nation on to its liberation. He has demonstrated that a powerful human following can be assembled not only through the cunning game of the usual political manoeuvres and trickeries but through the cogent example of a morally superior conduct of life. The admiration for Mahatma Gandhi in all countries of the world rests on recognition, mostly sub-conscious, recognition of the fact that in our time of utter moral decadence, he was the only statesman to stand for a higher level of human relationship in the political sphere. This level we must, with all our forces, attempt to reach. We must learn the difficult lesson that an endurable future of humanity will be possible only if, also in international relations, decisions are based on law and justice and not on self-righteous power, as they have been up to now.

Albert Einstein

His goodness is what made him great In Gandhiji there was no line between goodness and greatness. His goodness is what made him great. Gandhi's sign of forgiveness displayed towards the man who struck him down proved how close he reached the great ones who lived spiritually in tune with infinite goodness. Religion is the bond which, when viewed in relation to time, ties those who come after. Gandhi without religion and without the spirit would not be Gandhi. Gandhi now belongs to the ages. The new India arising will be an everlasting monument to his goodness, his greatness and his spirit.

Senator F. Thomas

Truly walked with God In the passing of the great disciple Gandhi, our common manhood has lost a kinsman. Probably no man since Christ has more devoutly or literally followed and lived out the teachings of the master of men than he whose memory we honour today. He was held in esteem and regard throughout the civilised world. Conscious of the greatness of his mission, he sacrificed himself for others imposing on himself rigid restrictions. Abstaining from fleshly lust which was against the soul, he truly walked with God in the world. With many great powers reverting to the law of the jungle, this man of God turned the sword of the spirit which is the word of God.

Senator Charles Tobey

I shall always regret that Mahatma Gandhi died before he had an opportunity to appear before the United Nations. It would, indeed, have been a time to remember—Gandhi, dressed in his simple way, disdaining ambition and affectation, quietly reminding the nations of the world that humanity is indivisible and that settle our differences we must.

Fred Rosec, Executive Director of the Asia Institute

He belongs to the ages Gandhi the Saint will be remembered not only on the plains and in the hills but all over the world. The power of his benignity grew stronger as his potential influence ebbed. He tried in the mood of the New Testament to love his enemies. Now he belongs to the ages. He has left as his heritage a spiritual force that must in God's good time prevail over arms and armaments and the dark doctrines of violence.

The New York Times

Not simply great but good Gandhi was not simply a great man, but a good man; and, as the sorrowing people of many nations will know, the combination of the qualities of greatness and goodness in the man is too rarely achieved and too little appreciated.

There have been too few such men in human history, and they have so often been sorely and cruelly dealt with by the men of their times.

So it has been with Gandhi who, loving all men and lending the infinite wisdom of his great mind and the incalculable greatness of his gentle spirit to the enrichment and enlightenment of his fellow-beings, is now destroyed, in a physical sense, by the insensate act of a man for whom, even the instant before death, the sign of forgiveness was made. But Gandhi is not destroyed, or his noble work or his beloved name or his honoured place in the affections of the world today and in the eternal annals of history.

It is only the life of Gandhi which is at an end, for there is no work of destruction which could be wrought against the edifice of kindness and dignity, reason and justice, which he patiently and selflessly created for the good of India and the peace of the world, hour upon hour, and day upon day, and year upon year, throughout the prolific time of his fruitful life.

Hearst chain of Newspapers

It should be a cause for rejoicing that so great and courageous a soul, consecrated to an ideal cherished by all men of goodwill, should have lived in our time to set an example that could well be the pattern for world peace.

The Richmond Times Dispatch

A universal saint Mahatma Gandhi's final greatness will be voiced not through the nation he sought to create but in the aspiring hearts of all men in all nations and at all times.

But let us start with the fact—Gandhi was not just a 'great man'—he was a universal saint, something the West had not produced for many generations.

Life

Quintessence of the man of peace There is still some hope for the world which reacted as reverently as it did to the death of Gandhi. The shock and sorrow that followed the New Delhi tragedy shows we still respect sainthood even when we cannot fully understand it. There are striking parallels between the life of Gandhi and Jesus as recorded in the New Testament. Like Jesus, Gandhi was the quintessence of the man of peace and like Jesus he met a violent death.

Albert Deusch of P.M., New York

One of the saviours of mankind The New York Times correspondent described him as "The greatest Indian since Buddha" and others referred to him as "The greatest man since Christ". These characterizations are elementary—they anticipate the sure judgment of posterity. I shall never cease to be grateful that I recognised this years ago—Gandhiji was to me the greatest of men and the noblest of spiritual prophets from the first moment that I knew him.

...Your father was not only the greatest but also the most lovable of men. I have felt in his death an acutely personal loss which has almost broken my heart. I know that in this I am sharing the feelings of all who have known him or even seen him. His hold upon men's souls was irresistible and his power therefore incredible. I am convinced that in his death he will be even more influential than in his life. He died for the noblest of causes, the reconciliation of all men in brotherhood and love and he must be remembered, as long as the world endures, as one of the saviours of mankind.

Rev. Dr John Holmes, Minister, Community Church, New York
(in a letter to Mr Devadas Gandhi)

SOUTH AMERICA

BRAZIL

This idealistic man did create a whole spirit preaching against violence.

Senator Jose Almeida, President, National Democratic Union

CHILE

He was the leader of the masses who wielded kindness as arms. His death is a loss for the spirit of the world which will be irreparable if the seed of his doctrines is not rooted in millions of hearts. I think the best homage we could render to his memory is the condemnation of violence of any kind.

Gabriel Gonzalez Videla, President

COLOMBIA

The death of Gandhi is a great loss not only to India, but to the whole world and the Colombian nation offers its heart-felt tribute to the memory of the illustrious dead for his signal services and his political and human virtues.

M. Marano Spina Bebez, President

PANAMA

Died a martyr to liberty Mahatma Gandhi who fought for years for the independence of India and who saw blood run through its streets, cities and fields, finally witnessed the enormous triumph of the separation of his country from the British Empire.

But his ideals did not receive the compensation of which they were entitled. He died a martyr to his dream of liberty months after attaining a triumph. The memory of Mahatma Gandhi merits the respect of all lovers of liberty.

With him has disappeared one of the greatest figures of this epoch, the standard-bearer of human ideals.

El Panama-America

PERU

If with you they want to kill peace in the world, they will find that it is still living in India and America with people who will follow your heroic example...No Mahatma Gandhi, you have just been born in the blood of all men with faith in your admirable acts.

La Tribuna

I must reduce myself to zero. So long as man does not of his own free will put himself last among his fellow creatures, there is no salvation for him. *Ahimsa* is the farthest limit of humility.

-Mahatma Gandhi

MIDDLE EAST AND AFRICA

ABYSSINIA (Ethiopia)

A moral leader of all humanity The tragic loss of Indian people's great spokesman... not only India but the whole world will mourn the passing of a great man and a moral leader for all humanity.

His Imperial Majesty Haile Sellassie, Emperor of Abyssinia

MOROCCO

Symbol of oppressed peoples' liberty The people of Morocco have learnt with consternation of the tragic end of the great Mahatma, symbol of liberty of all oppressed peoples and apostle of concord and human fraternity.

Ahmed Balafrej, Secretary-General, Rabat

RHODESIA (Zimbabwe)

Great Gandhi... The loss sustained by you and your people with the tragic passing away of Great Gandhi.

Prime Minister

SUDAN

The Sudan has been profoundly shocked by the news of the assassination of Mahatma Gandhi.

Governor-General

THE UNION OF SOUTH AFRICA

Prince among men Gandhi was one of the great men of my time and my acquaintance with him over a period of more than 30 years has only deepened my high respect for him. A prince among men has passed away and we grieve with India in her irreparable loss.

Field-Marshal Jan Smuts, ex-Premier

AFGHANISTAN

I do not know why people should destroy such lives, which live for ever in the memory of time.

Indians should try to keep up burning the candle he lighted in the spirit of peace, cherishing feelings of love and brotherhood and respecting individual rights and the demand for independence.

H.M. King Zahir Shah

Gandhi, the peace-loving patriot Mahatma Gandhi, the peace-loving, the most patriotic and the most beloved leader of the people of India.

Prime Minister

ARABIA

A great loss which hits both India and the whole of the East...

President, Arab Higher Committee

The world has lost a great man This is the worst crime that could possibly have been perpetrated against humanity. The world has lost a great man.

Azzam Pasha, Secretary-General of the Arab League

EGYPT

Sublime example of sacrifice I learn with most profound emotion of the tragic death of illustrious Mahatma Gandhi, whose pacific struggle for the triumph of his patriotic and humanitarian ideals will remain forever a sublime example of sacrifice and heroism.

H.M. King Farouk

The sad loss of the great spiritual leader of India whose lofty humanitarian ideals augured a new era of peace and progress for India and the world at large.

M. Nokrashy Pasha

Mahatma Gandhi consecrated and gave his life to an exalted human ideal. Egypt...was always a great admirer of his ideals.

M.A.F. Radwan, Egyptian Consul in Bombay

He served the cause of peace, not for one group, but for all.

M. Nahas Pasha, Wafdist Leader

His death is a great loss to humanity and to peace.

Rector, Al Azhar University

IRAQ

A Leader of all peace lovers Gandhi was the greatest leader of all peace lovers in the world. Gandhi's death is a loss not only to India but to humanity and the civilized world.

Regent

Gandhi has not died; his teachings will live for ever. I always regard Gandhi's teachings as the only way to lead the world to peace and security.

M. Hamdi Pachachi, Minister of Foreign Affairs

India has lost her greatest history-builder Mahatma Gandhi's death has shocked me. I regard the Mahatma as one of the greatest men who have ever lived. His death is not a loss to India alone but to the world. India has lost her greatest history-builder and the world has lost one of the greatest humanitarians who has continuously fought evil and has done his utmost for peace.

M. Kamil Chandrchi, Leader of the National Democratic Party, Baghdad

LEBANON

The noblest figure of modern history The loss of Mahatma Gandhi will be felt by entire humanity which has lost in his person the noblest figure of modern history.

President

PALESTINE

The world's noble guardian of humanity and universal righteousness.

President, General Council of the Vaadelumi, Jewish Community

SYRIA

A great patriot The death of this great patriot has thrown India in consternation.

President of the Council

Gandhiji did not die in vain His views may be respected perhaps even more after his death than in his life, and he will not have died in vain if the people of India are encouraged to continue in the ways of peace for which he sacrificed his life.

M. Faris Bey el Khoury, Syrian Member of the Security Council

SOUTH & EAST ASIA

BURMA (Myanmar)

I am shocked beyond words by news of Mahatma Gandhi's death. One of the greatest figures of the world has been laid low by the hand of an assassin.

President

The great saint and leader Mahatma Gandhi's death is regarded here as a loss also to the Burmese nation and today is, therefore, a day, of mourning for Burma. Burma renders to India at this supreme moment of our common grief her utmost sympathy at the irreparable loss of the great Indian saint and leader.

Thakin Nu, Premier

Villages in Burma pay homage A loss to Burma as it was to India, Mahatma Gandhi was a world figure, an apostle of truth and peace, and Burma mourns his loss deeply. Even in villages in Burma, people of all communities are holding meetings to pay homage to the great man.

U Tin Tut

A national loss to Burmans The world has suffered an irreparable loss today. The father of the Indian nation is now no more. He has become a victim of the forces of evil. We now see to what length such forces of evil will go. We are completely stunned by this most cowardly act and unexpected tragedy. Just as Jesus Christ suffered to save suffering humanity, so has the Mahatma suffered now.

To us, Burmans, it is more than a national loss, no less painful than the loss of our own leaders in last July. The Burmese people had a special reverence for the Mahatma. The world has lost its greatest man in history—the living personification of love and truth.

U Win, Burmese Ambassador to India

The wicked hand of the assassin may be blessed that it was instrumental for your great father to take his rank with other great martyrs of the world-Socrates, Jesus, Hassan and Lincoln.

Dr Ba Maw (in a letter to Devadas Gandhi)

His doctrine—a religion Even in his life-time there were indications that many of his followers regarded him not only as a saint but also as a founder of a religion, and final sacrifice was just what was necessary to make his doctrine a religion, and Mahatma a saviour of humanity from forces of evil which he fought all his life, such as, domination of one country over another, domination of caste, repression of the outcast and application of violence to human relations.

The Burmese Review, Rangoon

Mahatma Gandhi will be remembered as a foremost hero in the world's history of the last 2,000 years. No one after Gautama the Buddha has won such respect and honour from people as Mahatmaji.

The New Light of Burma, Rangoon

CEYLON (Sri Lanka)

Great and irreparable loss Please accept heart-felt and sincere condolences of the people and the Government of Ceylon and myself at the great and irreparable loss India and yourself have suffered by the untimely death of Mahatma Gandhi.

D. S. Senanayake, Prime Minister

The greatest figure of humanity There is no doubt Mahatma Gandhi's satyagraha movement helped Ceylon and other countries to achieve freedom. The Mahatma was the greatest figure of humanity since Buddha. He is perhaps the hoped for Maitreya Buddha.

W.H. de Silva, Special Representative of Ceylon in India

A leader of humanity India has lost her Father; the world has lost a leader of humanity. The Mahatma will be greater yet in death than life.

Sir Oliver Goonetilleke, High Commissioner in the UK

CHINA

Saintly crusader of peace It is, indeed, a heart-breaking tragedy that the saintly crusader of peace through nonviolence should fall a victim of violence.

Generalissimo and Madame Chiang Kai-shek

Mankind has lost one of its greatest leaders I was greatly shocked by the sudden and untimely death of Mahatma Gandhi. Not only India but all mankind has lost one of its greatest leaders..... His death will be an eternal inspiration to all fellow Asians to whom his life will forever be a source of pride.

Chang Chun, former Premier

Teacher of peace In his passing away India has lost an inspiring leader and the world a greater teacher of peace.

Wang Shieh-chieh, former Foreign Minister

A merciful father of the Indian people A merciful father of the Indian people and a spiritual teacher of mankind, Gandhiji had spent his whole life-time in seeking the deliverance of India and the world from the evil forces of violence, cruelty, selfishness and avarice...his teachings...will continue... to guide all nations towards a great awakening of conscience and an ultimate forging of universal brotherhood.

Dr Tai Chi Tao, President of the Executive Yuan and Dr Chu Chia-hua, Minister without Portfolio

He could think their thoughts...shed their tears Gandhiji discovered the uncommonness of common men and he was not happy unless he was with them. Dressed like one of them, eating their simple food, having no possessions like the poorest of men, he could thus think their thoughts, understand their wants and needs and laugh their laughs and shed their tears. He had become the crystallization of all the good traits and virtues of the Indian villagers. Gandhiji is dead. He lives for ever.

Dr Lo Chia-Luen, Chinese Ambassador to India

Worked with devoted self-denial for peace Few persons in the contemporary world have worked with such devoted self-denial for the cause of peace through peaceful methods. The people of the world in their endeavour for peace will derive inspiration from the great ideals which Mahatma Gandhi consecrated his life to achieve.

Dr Wellington Koo, Chinese Ambassador in Washington

One of the greatest men He was one of the greatest men in history... it is to be hoped that his martyrdom will hasten the accomplishment of the sacred task he left unfinished.

Dr Cheng Tein-hsi, Chinese Ambassador in London

He symbolised highest ideals of his people Mahatma Gandhi's death at the hands of an assassin just at the moment of India's freedom is a staggering loss to his people.

Mahatma Gandhi was the architect of India's freedom. Without his heroic leadership and sacrifice, the country would still be far from its goal. He symbolized in his own person the highest ideals of his people. The Mahatma was shot down while leading his last noble fight for India's unity. His death in the cause of a united India raised him to a pedestal of supreme greatness. China feels the loss with profound grief.

Mahatma Gandhi was a great Asiatic. His ideals will live after him as an inspiration to posterity.

Dr Hollington Tong, Director, Chinese Information Department

The only modern saint and prophet Mahatma Gandhi was the only modern saint and prophet which his country produced. Only in a country like India or in Asia could a man achieve tremendous political power because of spiritual power.

Indians must decide the possibility of war. I hope peace will prevail.

Such a phenomenon as Mahatma Gandhi could not be possible in the Western world. It should convince Westerners not to interfere in Oriental politics.

Lin Yu-tang, Chinese author and philosopher

Mankind's great loss The death of Mahatma Gandhi is mankind's great loss.

Dr Hu Shih, President, Peking National University

Spirit to enlighten mankind The spirit of Gandhiji may live for ever to enlighten mankind.

Ta Kung Pao (Chinese Newspaper)

INDO-CHINA

The death of the apostle of peace and non-violence is resented by all men of goodwill who in the war's troubled aftermath place their hopes in moral force. The Indo-Chinese and French peoples join in expressing their sorrow to the people of India.

M. Bollaert, French High Commissioner for Indo-China

INDONESIA

Irreparable loss to mankind It is not only an irreparable loss to India but to the whole of mankind.

Dr Soekarno, President

Messenger of peace and freedom He was the messenger of peace and freedom and we mourn his death as our own loss...May God give us wisdom to emulate his example.

Dr Mohammad Hatta, Vice-President

One of the greatest leaders One of the greatest leaders the world ever had as well as a great person has been lost. His far-seeing wisdom and peace-loving mind made him a source of courage not only for your people but for all people in need of guidance.

Dr Soedarsano, Representative of the Republic of Indonesia in India

Prophet of peace That the prophet of peace and nonviolence should meet his death in this way is a great tragedy for the world. We, Indonesians, who have long revered him for his life-long battle against oppression and misery, join whole-heartedly in mourning the loss of a leader who had during his long life-time become a living legend to us.

Dr Soebandrio, Representative of the Republic of Indonesia in Britain

World poorer The whole world has become poorer.

Dr Hubertus van Mook, Lieutenant Governor-General of the Netherlands East Indies

Epitome of all the best evolved by India In various periods of India's history great leaders of thought and men arose whose teachings and leadership not only affected India but the whole world.

I regard Mahatma Gandhi as the greatest figure of the twentieth century. He was an epitome of all the good and the best that India had evolved during many centuries.

Dr D.L. Friedmann, University of Indonesia, Batavia

JAPAN

I am deeply shocked by the news on Mahatma Gandhi. This is an event of great sorrow.

H.I.M. Emperor Hirohito

Great pacifist I had always had the deepest respect for Gandhiji's life-long devotion to the cause of Indian independence and freedom as well as world peace. It was especially tragic that such a great pacifist had fallen a victim to brute force and violence but I firmly believe that the will of the great Indian leader would be realised by the Indian people.

Tetsu Katayama, Prime Ministet

MALAYA

Only saint of the modern world Gandhiji was perhaps the only saint of the modern world, and certainly the only saint of modern nationalism and modern politics. In his long life of identification of himself with the poor and the oppressed at the lowest levels of Indian society; in the utter simplicity and selflessness of his personal life; in the gentleness and yet the firmness of his spirit; in his unflinching courage in fighting for causes in which he believed; in his indifference to ridicule, misrepresentation, malice and hostility; in his life-long search for inner peace and spiritual guidance amid the cross-currents of religious, racial, class and caste conflicts in India; in the constant and many-sided activity in the field of practical affairs which he carried on in spite of a frail body and poor health; and, above all, in his consistent preaching and practice of non-violence—in all those aspects of his life and personality, Gandhiji indubitably was a saint.

The Straits Times, Singapore

NEPAL

Peace to his sacred departed soul Myself, my brothers and the people of Nepal were greatly shocked to hear of the assassination of Mahatmaji. We pray to Almighty Rama to grant peace to his sacred departed soul.

H.M. The Maharaja of Nepal

PHILIPPINES

India's immortal son The Filipino people are shocked and grieved to hear of the dastardly assassination of India's immortal son and acknowledged architect of her freedom.

President

From the standpoint of Asiatic and world politics Mahatma Gandhi's assassination constitutes a definite setback for such nationalist movements as those in the Netherlands, East Indies, Indo-China and elsewhere.

Miles W. Vaughan, U.P.A. Far Eastern Manager

SEYCHELLES

Universal sorrow The people and the Government of Seychelles share the universal sorrow arising from the tragic and irreparable loss in the passing away of the Mahatma.

Governor

TIBET

The great apostle of peace I am extremely sorry to hear of the death of Mahatma Gandhi, the great apostle of peace.

The Dalai Lama

My Government have held special religious services and worship in the great temple of Lhasa in front of the image of our exalted Lord Buddha and offered one thousand each of five different kinds of offerings.

H.H. Takdak Pandit Hothokthu, Regent

AUSTRALIA

Worked for the good of humanity and ways of peace Mr Gandhi will be remembered in Australia as a man who worked for the good of humanity and ways of peace.

J.B. Chifley, Premier

Example will strengthen the cause of peace among all nations Peoples of all classes and creeds throughout the world join in mourning the loss of Mahatma Gandhi, the news of whose tragic death has shocked and saddened all Australians.

The Mahatma's part in the fashioning of modern India, in developing a sense of national consciousness culminating in the achievement of India's independence, throughout a long life of selfless service, are too well known to need recapitulation.

His. ceaseless efforts for the uplift of down-trodden humanity, and especially, the depressed classes, are only part of the secret of his unique hold upon the millions of his fellow countrymen. His loss will be felt more deeply than ever at the present critical juncture. Throughout his life he stood uncompromisingly for the elimination of violence in human relationship to which end his latest fast was a unique contribution.

The Australian people most sincerely wish and hope that Mahatma Gandhi will not have died in vain, that communal reconciliation and harmony will be brought nearer by his tragic death and that his example will strengthen the greatest cause of all—peace among all nations and peoples.

Dr Herbert Evatt, Deputy Prime Minister

The most remarkable man Many people outside India regard Mr Gandhi as a revolutionary but I only say that Mr Gandhi was one of the most remarkable men I have been privileged to meet.

R. G. Casey (former Governor of Bengal)

Mahatma's name a household word It will surely interest you in India to learn how Mahatma Gandhi was revered in Australia, in a country which has never seen him but knew him well through his books and from his pictures. It will be only in this way in the future, alas, that he will be known, even in India. Mahatma Gandhi, himself, was a simple and homely man. Although Mahatma Gandhi's name has been for years a household word in Australia where we have read of him in newspapers, seen his photographs and formed some idea of his great influence and prestige, it was not until we actually landed in India that we could fully appreciate the extent of that influence, particularly his spiritual influence, exercised upon the hearts of the people.

We Australians who have been in India during the recent vivid years of Mahatma Gandhi's life count ourselves fortunate to have had the privilege of meeting and talking with a man who, even now and more so by future generations, will be numbered among the greatest figures of world history.

Lt-Gen Sir Ivan Mackay, former Australian High Commissioner in India

UNO

He will still be a noble symbol A tragic event dominates our thoughts. We have met today under the spell of emotion which has gone through the world at the death of Mr Gandhi.

Mr Gandhi gave to the world a great lesson. Few people have shown such absolute devotion to the generous ideas to which he had vowed himself. On many occasions he offered the sacrifice of his life so that these ideas might triumph.

From the distance he appeared to us to be already above this world as a great symbol. He represented in the highest degree and in its most noble aspect the spirit of the independence of his people.

The death of Gandhi will not end his beneficial work. Gone from this world, he will still be the noble symbol which he was in life.

M. Fernand Van Langenhove (Belgium)

In the death of Mahatma Gandhi, Asia has lost her greatest living saint. No other man typified the wisdom and nobility of the old continent as Mahatma Gandhi. His principles had universal significance.

Dr T.F. Tsiang, Permanent Chinese Representative at UNO

As one of the outstanding leaders of India, Mr Gandhi has certainly left a deep mark on the history of India. The name of Mr Gandhi will always be linked with the struggle which the Indian people led over such a long period for their national liberation.

M. Gromyko (USSR)

Friend of the poorest, lowliest and the lost Mr Gandhi was a man whose greatness belonged not only to his life-time but history.

Some of the greatest men in human history have fallen by assassin's hands. Others, like Mr Gandhi, have known that their lives were menaced. None has shown such selfless contempt for danger. None in his death has shown so clearly how senseless and sterile is the act of murder, and the fanaticism from which it springs.

We believe that his greatest achievements are still to come. Mr Gandhi was the friend of the "poorest, the lowliest and the lost"

Philip Noel-Baker (UK)

It is tragic that this death has come at a time of tension and crises, when toleration is so badly needed. We earnestly hope that his martyrdom will inspire the peoples of the United Nations to press forward with greater determination the ideals for which he stood.

Senator Warren Austin (USA)

Keystone of the arch of peace Mr Gandhi's tragic death constitutes as grievous a loss to Pakistan as to India. Indeed, it is an irreparable loss to the cause of peace throughout the world.

Mr Gandhi was beloved by hundreds of millions and deeply reverenced by all who heard his name. One of his many claims to greatness was the faculty which always enabled him to win through to sanity in every one of the crises which he faced during his life.

The irony is that he should have fallen by the hand of an assassin. The poignancy and tragedy is enhanced by the realization that he was the keystone of the arch that is at this moment subject to so many stresses.

The keystone has been removed by a dastardly hand. It is difficult to assess what this disaster may portend. Yet one should be permitted to indulge the hope and utter the prayer that, through the supreme sacrifice, Mr Gandhi may have accelerated the achievement of those ideas for which his whole life was dedicated.

Sir M. Zafrullah Khan (Pakistan)

His life will be an inspiration and a beacon light. Our hearts are filled with unspeakable grief. A great tragedy has overtaken us; the greatest, perhaps, in Indian history in recent years.

His life will be a great inspiration to the people of India. It will serve as a beacon light to those races and nations who believe that force is not needed in human existence, that the highest achievement of the human race is only possible through non-violence.

If there was one man in the world who embodied in his life and conduct, who preached through all his life, the principles upon which the United Nations was founded, it was Mahatma Gandhi.

N. Gopalaswami Ayyangar (India)

No Frenchman but reveres his name With the death of Mr Gandhi, one of the greatest and finest figures of humanity has gone. There is not a Frenchman who did not know and revere the name of Mr Gandhi. He fell for his ideals and crowned a most noble life with a martyr's death.

M. Guy de la Tournelle (France)

Mr Gandhi convinced his followers that internal strife was not in the interests of the people, but in the interests of those who wanted to maintain the domination of India.

It is my hope and conviction that the death of Mr Gandhi will not halt the work of the Indian people in its struggle for a stable Government and the building up of their sovereignty.

M. Tarasenko (Ukraine)

Martyr in the cause of justice He proved by his life and preaching, the force and power of the spirit. He gave a great example to all.

He is the new martyr in the cause of justice. If we believe in his principles we may have confidence in the ultimate success of our work.

Dr Jose Arce (Argentina)

The death of Mr Gandhi is a catastrophe not only for India but for men of goodwill everywhere. In our sorrow at his passing, we who share his aspirations can only hope his influence will ever widen and harmonize men's minds in search for peace and freedom.

Gen Andrew McNaughton (Canada)

Set an example of unselfish devotion to the cause of humanity

Humanity at large, by one cruel blow, has been deprived of a great leader. Mahatma Gandhi, by his life and work, set an example of unselfish devotion to the cause of humanity. His influence was that of a great spiritual force inspiring men to nobler aims...we are moved...by a sense of the loss suffered by all mankind.

L.D. Wilgress (Canada), Chairman UN Conference, Trade and Employment

He will survive as an immortal symbol of understanding between men in the world torn with misunderstanding.

Dr. Julian Huxley, Director-General of UNESCO

Death is a true friend. It is only our ignorance that causes us grief.

-Mahatma Gandhi